SHAMANISM

SPIRITUAL GROWTH • HEALING • CONSCIOUSNESS

Publisher & Creative Director: Nick Wells
Editorial Director: Catherine Taylor
Copy Editor: Anna Groves
Art Director: Mike Spender
Digital Design & Production: Chris Herbert

Special thanks to: Dawn Laker, Frances Bodiam
and the artists who allowed us to reproduce their work.

FLAME TREE PUBLISHING
6 Melbray Mews, Fulham,
London SW6 3NS, United Kingdom
www.flametreepublishing.com

First published 2020

20 22 24 23 21
1 3 5 7 9 10 8 6 4 2

ISBN: 978-1-83964-199-2

A copy of the CIP data for this book is available from the British Library.

Printed in China | Created, Developed & Produced in the United Kingdom

SHAMANISM

SPIRITUAL GROWTH • HEALING • CONSCIOUSNESS

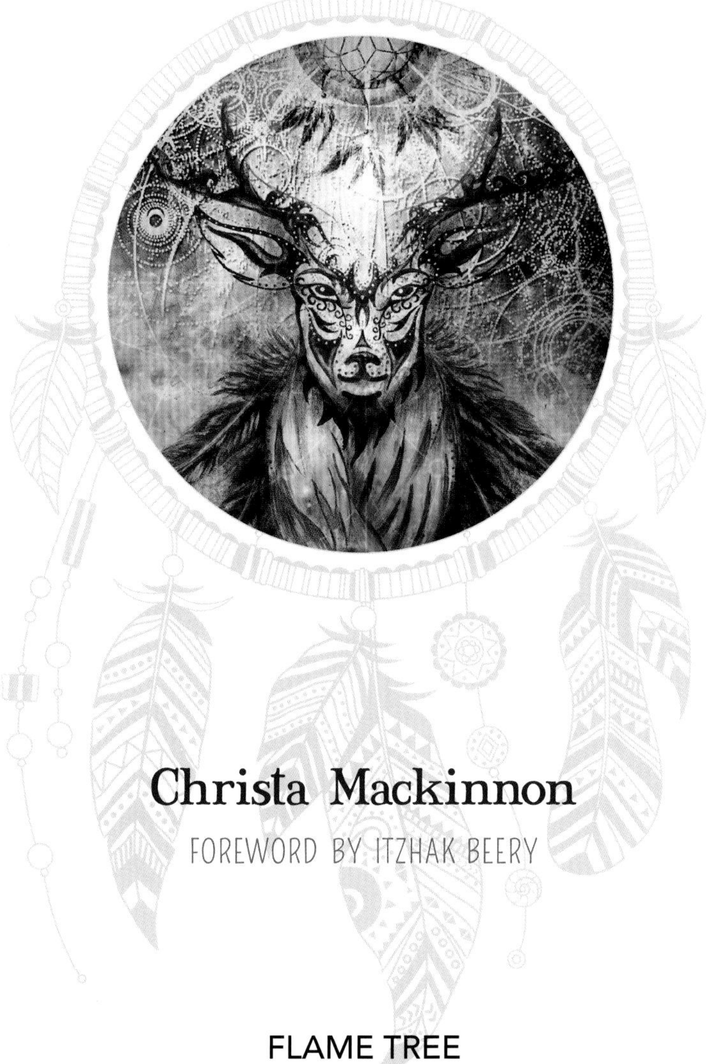

Christa Mackinnon

FOREWORD BY ITZHAK BEERY

FLAME TREE
PUBLISHING

CONTENTS

FOREWORD

One summer day, in 1995, through pure serendipity, I pulled a book from a bookstore shelf. That changed my life. I started down a fascinating and transformative shamanic path that took me on to many continents to meet amazing teachers, heal many thousands of people, lecture and write my books. I invite you to join me on this journey. Christa Mackinnon's striking book can change your life if you let your heart open and pay heed to your soul.

What is Shamanism?

My teacher, Ipupiara, always said, 'We are all shamans'. Humans have the innate skills to dream, vision, sense, hug, sing and speak words of comfort. At the same time, we have intelligence to realize the true nature of Nature. We are all born to heal each other and ourselves using the tools of the seen and unseen worlds.

Shamans do that by entering into a trance-like state of consciousness. They meet their invisible forces or spirit helpers – power animals, spirits of nature, ancestors or other teachers – by using drumbeat, voice, movement, playing music or the use of hallucinogens to retrieve and share information that otherwise cannot be obtained.

Information materializes in the language of the heart – poetry, creativity and intuition. It subverts our sceptical mind by using symbols, idioms, allegories, art and metaphors. In beautiful settings shamans create rituals and ceremonies, for all stages of life, with prayers, chants, sounds, dance, storytelling, sacred objects, masks, fire and more. We can open our hearts to the mystery, to exploring new possibilities, to re-experiencing nature, which will reunite us with our soul purpose and yearnings, to be part of the grand cosmos.

Shamanism is a time-tested practice, which allowed our ancestors to live in harmony with nature. I believe this cumulative sacred knowledge, from the time we set foot on Mother Earth, is crucial nowadays to heal ourselves in our troubled modern life.

ITZHAK BEERY

Founder of ShamanPortal.org

and The Andes Summit

WHY SHAMANISM & WHY NOW?

Today, people from all walks of life are becoming interested in shamanism, the oldest spiritual path known to humanity and one that offers us healing, the expansion of our consciousness, a reconnection to earth and spirit as well as personal evolution.

This renewed interest is connected to the growing awareness of the harm we have done to our environment and the damage we do to our own psyche by separating ourselves from nature, the mystical and sacred, and from community. Our souls need to be nourished and we instinctively feel that the shamanic can help us to lead more fulfilled, natural and soul-centred lives. We also recognize that we can benefit from the ecological skills, knowledge and teachings of those who have preserved earth-centred traditions.

If we go far enough back in our ancestry, we all come from tribal societies. Humans have lived in

communities that are close to nature much longer than in this urbanized technological world, and so the shamanic has remained within our psyche in various forms such as the healer, the visionary, the artist and the witch. These archetypes are now, more than ever, ready to be awakened.

My own journey into shamanism began over 20 years ago. Having established myself as a respected psychologist, therapist and university lecturer, I increasingly turned to shamanism as it offered transpersonal, spirit-orientated and consciousness-enhancing teachings that are often missing in modern psychology. Although I had been an explorer of the human psyche all my professional life, it took walking a shamanic path to finally come home.

Walking a shamanic path proved to be an enchanting, sometimes challenging, but unquestionably life-enhancing and magical experience. Its rich tapestry offers something to each of us on our journey towards what psychoanalyst Carl Jung called 'our soul discovering its meaning' and another psychologist, Abraham Maslow, called self-actualization. In shamanism we could call this 'becoming all that we can be, connected to all there is'. No matter which of the many shamanic pathways we choose, it supports us in the quest for wholeness through connecting us with the vast, deep layers of our own consciousness and the wider fields of existence.

'Not only is the shamanic type emerging in our society, but also the shamanic dimension of the psyche itself.'

THOMAS BERRY

WHAT IS SHAMANISM?

Shamanism is a spiritual practice that has endured since ancient times. It developed globally as our ancestors' way of exploring, living with, relating to and utilizing universal, natural forces within and around them. Rather than being a religion based on set teachings and practices, shamanism has always been an evolving spiritual system, taking a variety of forms in different cultures and at different times.

'No one culture or group of cultures has a hold on what is "shamanic". Shamanism is a group of skills to peer into other worlds and utilize the intelligence and forces of Creation to bring us to greater wholeness, clarity and self-realization.'

ZACCIAH BLACKBURN

Shamanism: A Universal Spiritual Path

Despite its many variations, shamanism is a universal path, as all shamanism originated in tribal societies and all shamanic practice and knowledge are based on expanding consciousness by entering altered states (trance states) to explore, connect and work with the 'hidden spirit worlds'. These spirit worlds, which we now might call 'the energetic quantum realms' or 'planes of consciousness', lie beneath and beyond what

is materially visible. Independently from each other, shamans all over the globe have for millennia described and utilized the spirit worlds in remarkably similar ways.

Shaman: An Umbrella Term

The word 'shaman' derives from the word *šaman*, which in the Evenki language of the Tungus tribe in Siberia means 'one who is excited, moved, raised, ecstatic' and also 'one who knows'. It is a gender-neutral term that was first spread by explorers who encountered traditional Siberian šamans. Over time it became an umbrella term for practitioners of nature-based traditions all over the world, who, in one form or another, travel to the spirit worlds to explore and work with them. Examples include the medicine men and women of North America, the curanderos of South America, the sangomas in Africa, the mudang in Korea or the kupuna in Hawaii. Then there are the many contemporary shamanic practitioners, who are not directly embedded in a particular tradition – they sometimes call themselves 'shamans', but in many cases prefer the term 'shamanic practitioner', so as not to imply that they are traditionally trained.

The Power and Magic of Shamanism

The power and magic of shamanism lies in its ability to connect us with 'all there is', with the vast and deep layers of the inner and outer realities, aiding us in our individual and collective evolution towards 'all that we can be'.

'Shamanism is essentially a living tradition of alchemy that is not seeking the stone but has found the stone.'

TERENCE MCKENNA

Shamanism Is a System of Connection

Shamanism connects all the worlds, the spiritual with the material, and our body and mind with our soul and spirit. It connects the human being with the earth, with community and with the wider fields of past, present and future, whilst enabling us to access the help, information and wisdom in those fields – from entities that include spirit guides, animal helpers and ancestral forces. It is, in that sense, holistic.

Shamanism Brings Us Back to Nature

As well as connecting us with nature, shamanism unites us with our own deeper nature. In a disconnected, artificial world, research by psychologists has shown that the drastic increase in mental disorders and emotional suffering is partly linked to our extreme

disconnection from the natural world. Shamanism reconnects us both to nature and to our own nature, embedding us within it, nourishing our earth-soul and leading us back to what is important in life.

Shamanism Expands Our Consciousness

By expanding our consciousness, shamanism enriches our mental world. As shamanic practices often lead us into altered states of perception, they provide us with extraordinary experiences and open deep inner and outer worlds. In the process, our consciousness expands and our view of the world and ourselves changes. It also provides guidance about what we experience when we are in such trance states and how to use them for healing, growth and the increase of our personal power.

Shamanism Brings a Sense of the Sacred into Our Lives

An African shaman in a small, materially poor village once said to me, 'You are the poorest people on earth, because you have lost the sacred and the mystical.' Shamanism understands that without the sacred, enchanting, magical and mystical, we are bound to lead impoverished lives. If we focus solely on the material, we are left with little sense of purpose and of being embedded into something bigger than ourselves. Shamanism reconnects us with the sanctity of life, with mystical experiences and with an enchanted state of being.

Shamanic Approaches Are Active and Involved

The shamanic engages our whole being. This applies to physical activities, such as when we create altars and mesas, trance dance, craft ceremonial objects and participate in ceremonies, attempt vision quests, enjoy drumming circles, go to community camps or reconnect with nature. It also applies to the more imaginal, such as when we journey, retrieve souls, pray or bless. All of this brings us into direct contact with the underlying fields and enables us to be the ecstatic co-creators that we are by our very nature.

TRADITIONAL SHAMANISM & SHAMANS

When we refer to traditional shamanism, we usually mean shamanism that has been – and still is – practised in tribal indigenous societies, or stems directly from such traditions. Our knowledge about these practices comes from many sources around the world.

Examples of these sources include cave arts and excavations, symbolism and rituals passed down through the ages, indigenous creation stories and, from the sixteenth century onwards, accounts from

'Shaman is a spiritual shuttle between three realms of existence: Heaven, Mankind and Earth. He pierces through inter-dimensional veils in order to heal the parts and unite the whole.'

LADA RAY

explorers. From the twentieth century onwards, studies and interviews with shamans have been undertaken by anthropologists, ethnologists, botanists, historians and psychologists. Completing the picture are tales from spiritual seekers and many accounts from living shamans stemming from long traditions.

The Making of Traditional Shamans

Indigenous tribal female and male shamans either came from lineages or were called by spirit to become shamans. The calling often occurred during a long crisis or illness, during which the person turned into an apprentice, enduring a severely altered state of mind and out-of-body experiences that tested their ability to work with the spirits and learn from them. Their training was usually (and still is) an intense affair, which includes profound initiation rites, often leading the apprentice into near-death experiences, in order to learn how to travel to the spirit worlds without being pulled back into the body by survival instincts and to work with all the spiritual forces, be they benevolent or malevolent.

The Skills and Powers of Traditional Shamans

Traditional shamans, while not a homogenous group, have had and still have certain characteristics and traits in common:

'Underneath the masks, the elaborate ceremonial clothing, the outrageous trance dancing, the astonishing shape shifting, the seizure-like movements and the spirit possessions of traditional shamans, we find indeed highly skilled, profoundly trained and experienced women or men, respected by their tribes.'

CHRISTA MACKINNON

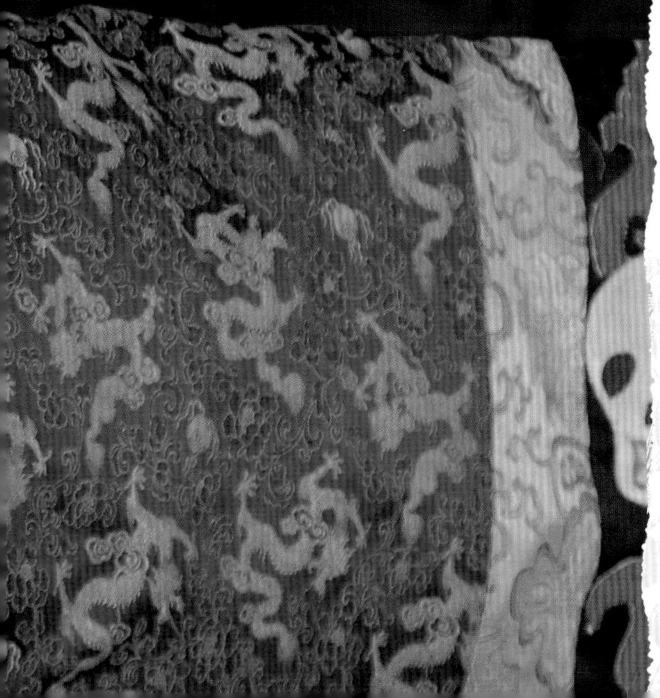

- **They are healers** of body and soul, visionaries, ritualists, psychics, divinatory practitioners, psychopomps, artists, shapeshifters and co-creators.
- **They are interdependent** with nature, spirit and their communities.
- **They are powerful**, knowledgeable and skilled utilizers of expanded states of consciousness and experts of the hidden spirit worlds.
- **They access those hidden worlds** and work within them for the benefits, health and harmony of the community and its individual members.
- **Their work bridges** the energetic spirit worlds and the material world.
- **To alter their states** of perception and access those worlds they use a variety of means: rhythmic instruments, such as drums and rattles; mantra-like sounds and songs; voice-like instruments such as flutes and whistles; meditative approaches; trance dances; rituals and ceremony; nature observation and communication; vision quests; lucid dreaming; psychoactive plants and more.

CONTEMPORARY SHAMANISM

Although traditional shamanism provides a solid basis for contemporary approaches, modern-day shamanism includes countless strands, varieties and combinations. Generally, it is a mixture of the traditional and the new and can be roughly divided into three practices.

'What's really important about shamanism is that there is another reality that you can personally discover.'

MICHAEL HARNER

Pure Uninterrupted Practices

We still find traditional shamanic practices all over the world, but in their purest forms only in regions that were remote enough to escape colonizing forces and missionaries and avoided interruptions of their traditions by being criminalized by so-called 'civilizing' political systems. Examples of uninterrupted practices can be found in tribes in the deep Amazon, in remote Siberia or on distant islands such as the Mentawai Islands in Indonesia.

Revived Traditional Practices

Most shamanic practices went underground for long periods, or were almost wiped out during the persecution and elimination of indigenous cultures around the world. The regions affected ranged from

the Americas, Australia and Africa, from Europe via Scandinavia to Siberia, Mongolia and all regions of Central and East Asia such as Korea and the Philippines. Over the last few decades we have seen remarkable rediscoveries and revivals of these ancient traditions, spreading to urban areas and being included in the healing systems of their countries and taught to people around the world.

Neo-Shamanic Practitioners and Teachers

Today there are countless non-indigenous, Western and urban shamanic practitioners worldwide. Some were trained and subscribe to one tradition, such as the Huichol or Toltec traditions from Mexico, the Huna tradition from Hawaii, the Nepalese Himalayan traditions (which strongly influenced Buddhism),

the Tengrism of Mongolia, or the Celtic and North European traditions as exemplified by the Norse or Sami people. Many others use eclectic mixtures of shamanic teachings and practices, adjusted to our times and the current state of the human psyche. The range of contemporary practitioners is somewhat narrower, specializing in areas such as shamanic healing, facilitating ceremonies, psychopomp work, journeying, soul retrieval or plant-based medicine.

Neo-shamanic practices share most of the defining features of traditional shamanism. They share a world-view and cosmology, they work in altered states and focus on the underlying energies, utilizing spirit allies. Their healing work is towards wholeness, with soul and spirit being seen as paramount. They also work with the natural world and for the community – although communities are of a different nature these days – and they use many of the tools traditional shamans use.

ANOTHER REALITY: HOW SHAMANISM SEES THE WORLD

The worldview of shamanism stems from experiencing and exploring reality within altered states of perception, from work in the spirit worlds and from the wisdom and knowledge passed on over time.

'Even the most primitive tribes have a larger vision of the universe, of our place and function within it, a vision that extends to celestial regions and space and to interior depths of the human in a manner far exceeding the parameter of our world of technological confinement.'

THOMAS BERRY

Everything Is Alive and Has Spirit

The shamanic view of the world is first and foremost animistic. This means that the universe and everything within it are seen as being alive and vibrational in essence. Together all living beings

form the web of life, also sometimes called 'all there is'. On these underlying essence levels, everything contains specific vibrational fields, which in shamanism is called 'spirit'. In more modern terms it could be called a quantum essence, frequency, a potentiality or consciousness.

Everything Is Connected and Evolving

As these underlying fields are connected, we can access, explore, communicate, utilize and work with them. Or, in other words, everything within the web influences us and can be influenced by us, as well as teach and support us. These essences – these life-force energies – are potentialities in a state of 'evolving and becoming'. This means that everything has an inbuilt drive to evolve, trying to reach the highest level of its potentiality. A very simplified example might be a tree essence: contained energetically in the seed, it has the drive to develop into a complete tree. A human essence has the drive to develop into a complete human.

Everything Comes from the Same Source

Shamanism assumes that there is a source from which all life-force essence stems. This source is seen as being undivided, whole and sacred. Everything is

'Humans are a part of creation and shamanism is our way of connecting with the whole.'

WILL ADCOCK

already inherent in potential form within that source, but we are unable to define it, hence it is often described as the 'Great Mystery' or 'Great Spirit'. As everything stems from this source, all of life is defined as being sacred.

A Brief Look at the Human Being

The human being is just one of the many life forms, albeit a complex one with the power to co-create. We have spirit as our essence and an individual soul, both underlying the body/mind. The soul carries the knowing of our spirit essence and our potentiality. It also carries the imprints of our individual and collective life experiences. Whilst our spirit essence is eternal, everyone's stemming from the same source, our soul can be harmed, shattered and contaminated. Soul loss (for example through trauma), undernourishment of our soul, and living out of balance with our soul's drive to evolve to our highest level are all highly damaging and underlie many mental and physical issues.

Some teachings divide the human soul into an 'earth soul' and a 'celestial soul', but no matter which view we subscribe to, in shamanism soul and spirit are seen as paramount, and shamanic healing work is therefore mainly concerned with the level of the psycho-spiritual.

SHAMANIC REALMS: LOWER, UPPER & MIDDLE WORLDS

Shamanism divides the underlying essence worlds, also called 'hidden worlds', into three basic levels: the lower world (or underworld), the upper world (or higher plane) and the middle world (our manifested world). As I have already said, shamans explore and work within all the worlds, accessing them by utilizing trance states.

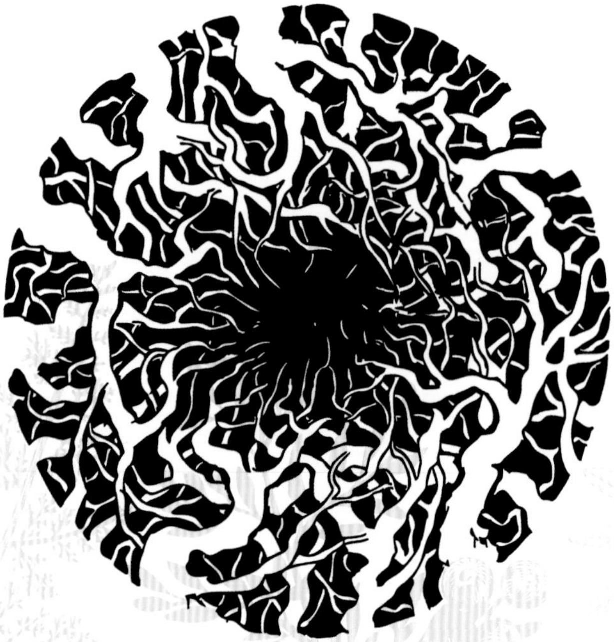

'Our normal [...] consciousness, rational consciousness [...], is but one type of consciousness, whilst all about it, parted by the flimsiest of screens, there lie potential forms of consciousness entirely different.'

WILLIAM JAMES

The Lower World

The lower world, or underworld, is purely energetic in nature. In trance states it is mostly experienced as a landscape, with mountains, deserts, forests, rivers, oceans, caves, valleys, jungles or combinations of these. It is the home of the spirits of animals as well as human-like, earth-connected spirits.

We access the lower world via a journey through an imagined opening or gateway into the earth, such

as the roots of the cosmic tree, tunnels or caves. The knowing we receive within the lower world is instinctual. It appears in strong images, sudden insights, emotional and physical reactions and, most importantly, it will be shown and taught to us by the spirit helpers of the lower world, the most significant ones being power animals.

The lower world is also concerned with the human psyche, with our unconscious. We generally find that our cut-off shadow aspects as well as our split-off soul parts reside there. The stories of the underworld are myths and fairy tales in which the hero or heroine may encounter dark forces, as frightening, devious, evil and monstrous beings populate the lower world.

Shamans work regularly in the lower world and have extensive knowledge of it. They have devised many ways, such as rituals, journeying, prayers and soul retrieval, to work with the lower-world energies to transform, heal and integrate them.

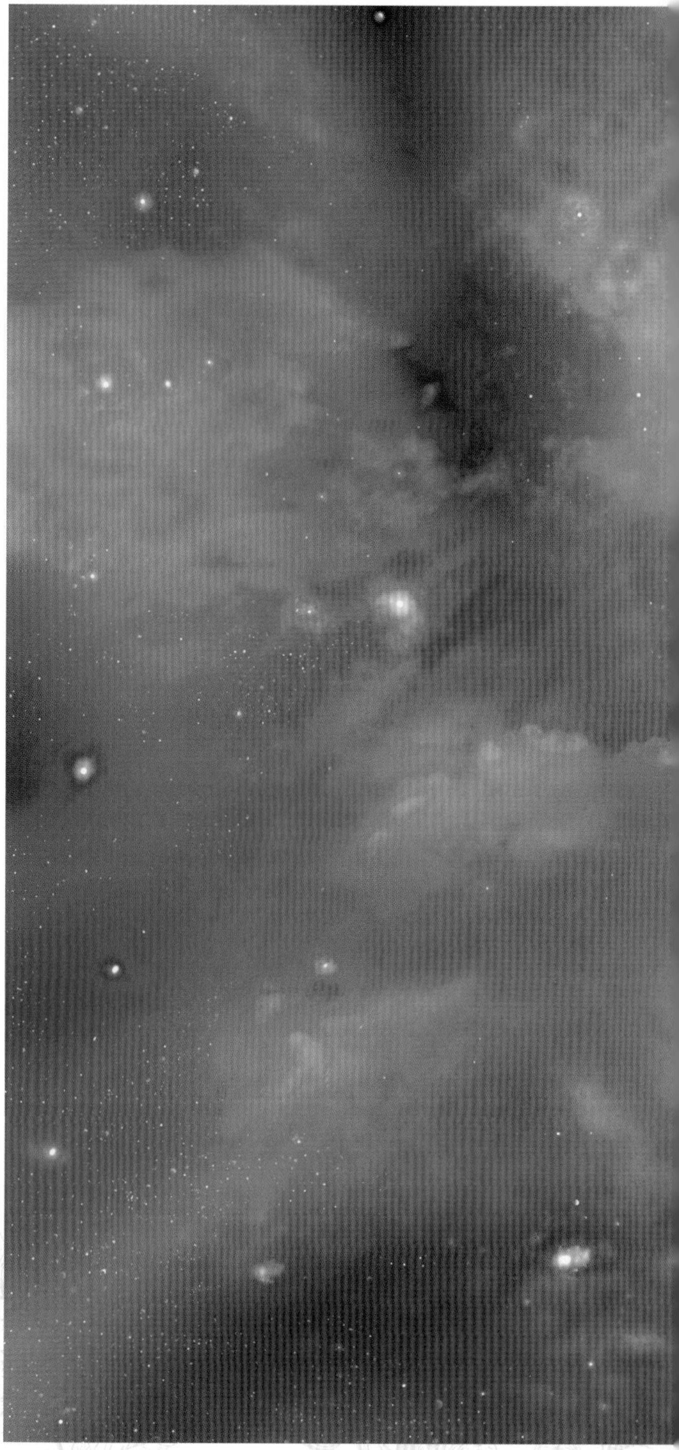

Shamans explore and work within all the worlds, utilizing them for guidance, wisdom and creation.

CHRISTA MACKINNON

The Upper World

The upper world is also energetic and traditionally accessed via the branches of the cosmic tree, staircases leading upwards, high mountains, rainbows or smoke. The upper world appears as an etheric, cloud-like realm of many layers, feeling quite airy, showing soft, fuzzy colours and crystal-like structures.

The upper world is inhabited by helping spirits, such as powerful teachers in humanoid form, entities and spirits that have never been in a body, as well as ancestral spirits. Here we seek guidance and

wisdom from spirit guides and teachers. What we perceive and receive is not instinctual, but rather has philosophical and wise qualities which reach beyond what we 'know'.

We can also look for our own 'higher self' within the upper world. This is our transpersonal aspect, which in some teachings is called the 'celestial soul', seen as the immortal aspect of ourselves with which we can communicate to access a source of intuition, inspiration and guidance.

The Middle World

The middle world is our manifested, material reality as well as the underlying energetic forces that create the material world. Here we explore, experience and communicate with the spirits of all that is manifested – the spirits of the plants, rocks, trees, waters, fire, earth and more. The middle world also encompasses the 'hidden folk', such as fairies, elves, trolls, stone guardians in stone circles and all the creatures described in fairy tales and folk myths.

The middle world is accessed via altered states focusing on the underlying essences of the material natural world, such as the plants, trees, mountains and elements. In the middle world we also focus on hunches, omens and synchronicities and we can attempt, for example, distant viewing or time-travelling.

SPIRITS & SPIRIT ALLIES OF THE SHAMANIC WORLDS

Whilst spirits can be either malevolent or benevolent, spirit allies are forces that provide guidance, power, help, wisdom and protection, essential in shamanic work. They are numerous, reside in all the worlds and are available to everybody. Here I will describe the most essential ones for shamanic work as well as for anyone who wants to walk a shamanic path, expand consciousness and access the help available to us.

'The shaman does not believe in a division between the body and the spirit or between the visible world of form and the invisible world of energy.'

ALBERTO VILLOLDO

Power Animals of the Lower World

Power animals are crucial in shamanism. They are the guardian spirits of the lower world, helping, protecting and possessing powerful teachings and knowledge, especially of the underworld. Being part of the divine energy of nature as well as the instinctual aspects of our earth souls in their natural state, the integration of power animals strengthens our instinctual knowing and reactions, embeds us further into the field of our earth soul, and provides us much help when tackling challenging emotional issues.

In indigenous cultures, animal totems are more than symbolic representations of traits such as courage, ferocity, agility or softness; they are seen as vital for a person's physical, mental and spiritual health and power. For example, in some cultures it is assumed that the spirits of at least two power animals accompany us from birth to keep us safe and healthy. Disconnection from them is seen as one of the causes of illness, with reconnection being vital to restore health.

For shamanic practitioners the assistance of various power animals is essential for tasks such as journeys to the lower world, healing, shapeshifting, ceremony and soul retrieval. Shamanic practitioners therefore develop intense and respectful relationships with them.

All power animals are equal and provide specific medicines, powers and abilities. The little mouse, carrying the medicine of looking closely at the 'small things' and analysing, is as powerful as the jaguar, which represents the medicine of courage, strength, fearlessness and seeing in the dark underworld. Which medicine we need depends on who we are, which energies we need to reconnect with and what we undertake at given moments in time.

Teachers and Guides of the Upper World

Spirit teachers and guides of the upper world can appear to us in humanoid, symbolic or energetic form. Inhabitants of the upper world can be spirit entities that have been in a body, such as ancestral spirits or ascendant masters, or that have never been in human form, such as light entities or 'archetypal' energies. As beings of the upper world, they are of a different vibration, having a mostly ethereal quality.

Upper world teachers and guides are allies who carry wisdom and knowledge. They can help us to see

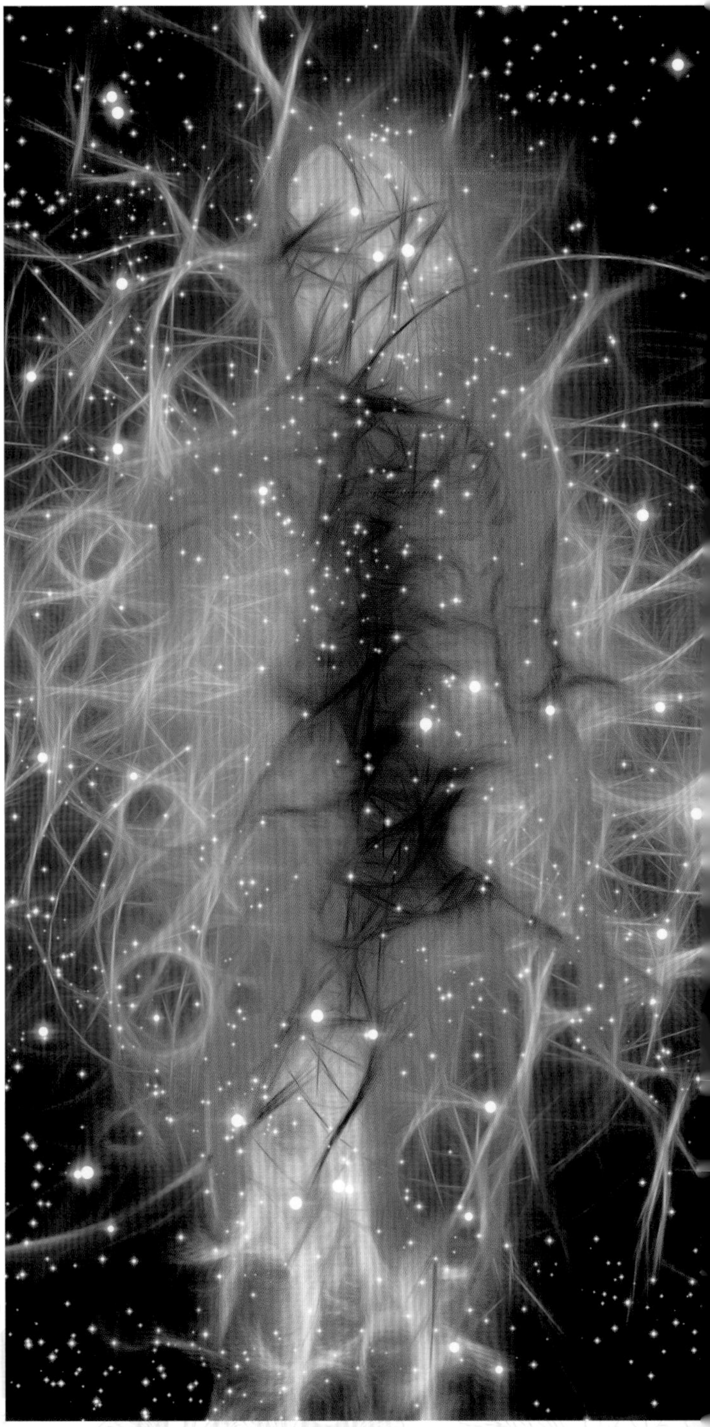

the bigger picture and can guide and teach us about subjects concerned with soul, purpose and meaning, as well as assist in healing, divination, ceremony and the energetic work we do in the different worlds.

Shamans often have several such allies, each with different qualities, roles and functions. They can be acquired through journeying into the upper world, ingestion of plant medicines, initiation ceremonies or dreaming.

Nature Spirits of the Middle Worlds

One of the objectives of shamanic work is to re-embed us into nature and regain lost knowledge, which we can receive by reconnecting to and interacting with the spirits of nature. Everything in nature, as I have already explained, is vibrational in essence, with spirit at its core. Shamanic practitioners work with the underlying fields of nature, with the spirits of water, earth, fire and air, with rivers, stones, stars, trees, plants, animals and mountains. They tune into their energetic fields, communicate with them, learn from them and utilize them in order to create healing, gain knowledge, and maintain balance and harmony. By reconnecting ourselves with nature and the spirits of nature we nourish our earth soul, we heal and we connect back to the source of our being and to what is important.

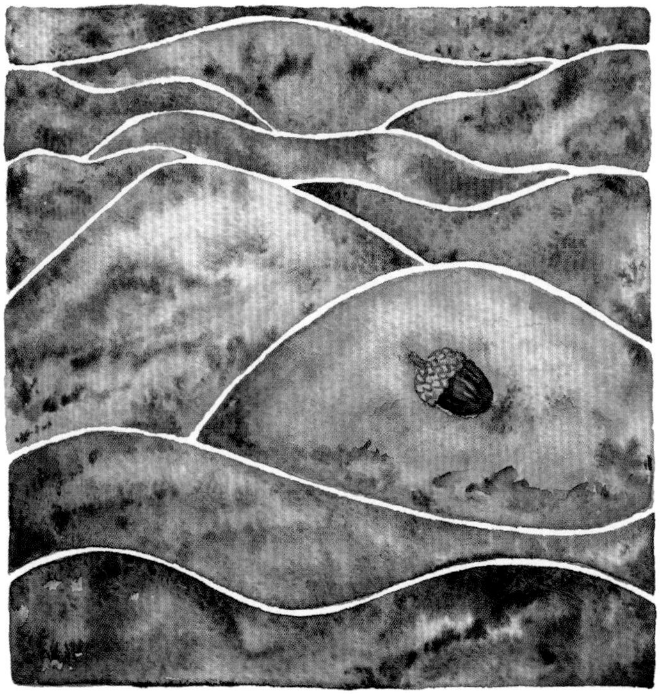

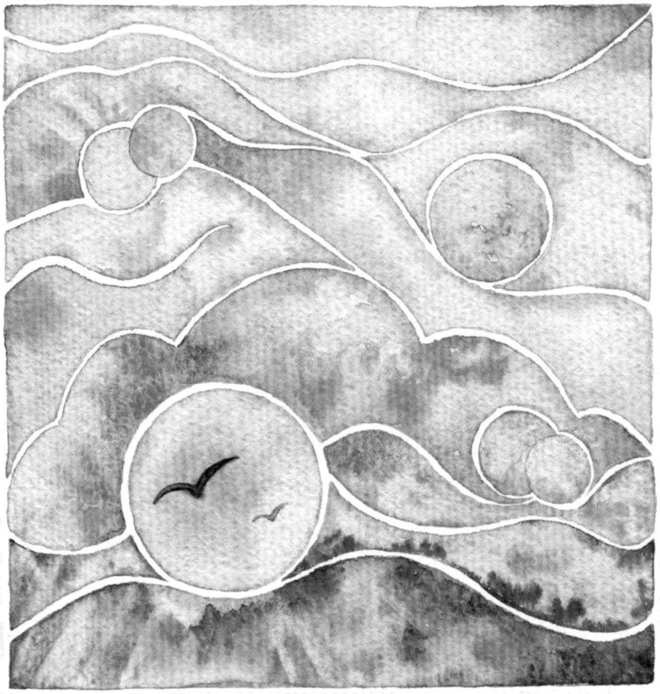

WALKING A SHAMANIC PATH TOWARDS WHOLENESS

So far in this book I have provided you with an overview of shamanism. From here onwards I will focus on walking a shamanic path and the various ways, teachings and techniques used in shamanism, including exercises you can use to start your own journey into shamanism.

With soul and spirit being seen as paramount, walking a shamanic path includes the integration of the various facets of ourselves, connecting to the wider fields of spirit and expanding consciousness. All of the means employed in shamanism help facilitate this. Whilst walking the shamanic path, we heal, find our purpose that is in alignment with the wishes of spirit and utilize our co-creative powers for the greater good of all of life.

'The shamanic is a journey and a path. It is a journey towards healing in the classical sense of "hal", meaning wholeness. It is a path to explore, connect with and integrate "all there is".'

CHRISTA MACKINNON

TWO BASICS: INTENT & ENERGY

Whilst walking a shamanic path over time sharpens our dual awareness of the material world and the underlying spirit worlds, we rarely access the spirit worlds directly and consciously without intent. An intent is a reason, a kind of outcome that we want to achieve. At its most potent, the intent bridges the energetic and the material.

'Intent is what sends a shaman through the wall, through space, through infinity.'

CARLOS CASTANEDA

An intent is more than a statement. It is a heartfelt desire, a focus and a direction. Let's say I want to

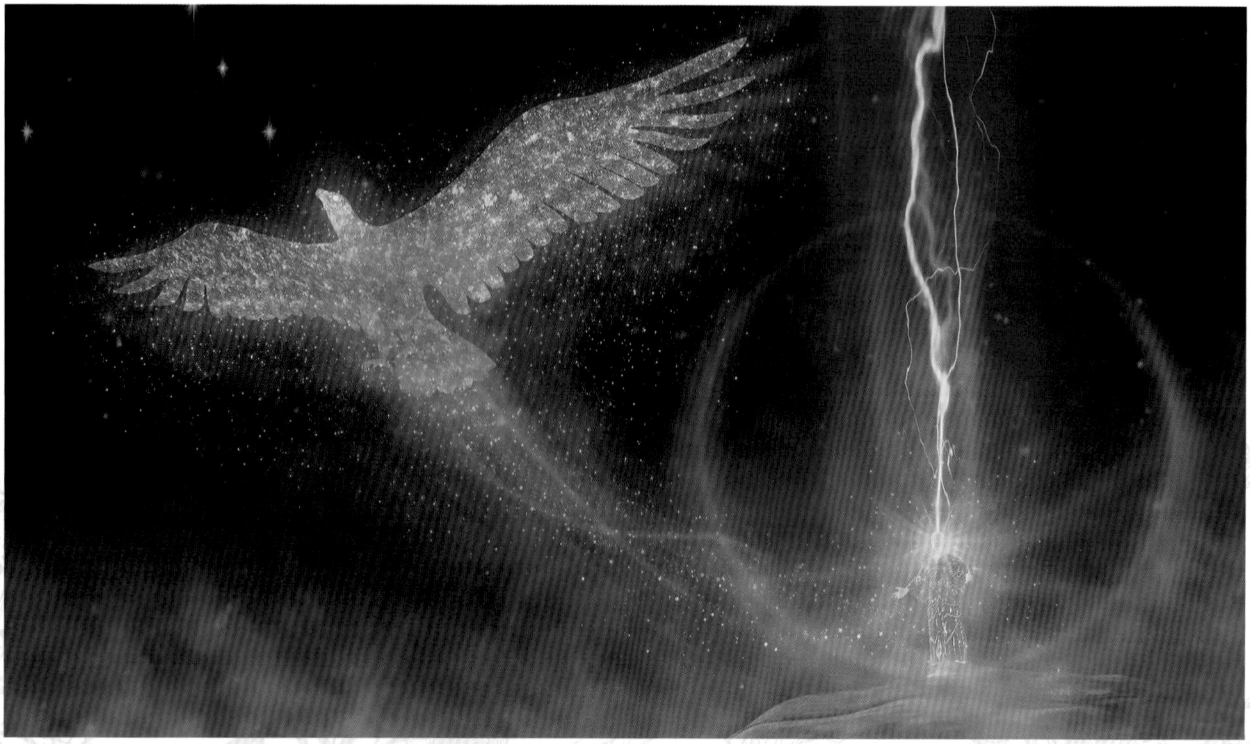

create a ceremony. What I want to achieve with the ceremony will direct the set-up, the spirits I evoke and the ritual I employ. For example, if the intent of the ceremony is to give thanks, the set-up would differ from that of a 'letting go' ceremony. As I will show you later, your intent directs your imagination, the pathway and the outcome of a shamanic journey. The intent directs the energies of all shamanic undertakings, which is why very powerful shamans can heal body and mind purely through intent.

'The universe doesn't speak English. It speaks frequencies.'

ANON

The shamanic worldview is energetic and therefore awareness of energies is fundamental. Whether we call spirit, set an intent for our work, journey, attempt healing or work with spirit allies, in shamanism we are always aware that we translate energetic forces. This applies to the forces we perceive and receive as well as to the ones we send out.

For most of us, the energies we work with translate into images, words, feelings, stories, hunches, body sensations, sudden insights, voices and synchronicities. Working with energies therefore requires knowledge,

practice, trust and the involvement of all our senses. Some of us are 'seers', who can see pure energies such as auras, but many are not. Kinesthetics, for instance, feel energies in their bodies, auditory people often hear voices, whilst more visually inclined people receive strong and clear images. Most of us experience a mixture of these and learn to trust our insights.

Cleansing Energy Fields

A good way to begin to develop awareness of, and work with, energies and intent is to cleanse energy fields and create beneficial ones. As fields can become contaminated, in shamanism we cleanse our own fields (aura), the space around us and the objects we work with, for ourselves and when we work. We also use cleansing to restore physical, mental and emotional balance, build energetic shields and to create and restore sacred space.

In shamanic practice this is done via smudging, which is the burning of herbs for cleansing, purification, protection, the banishment of negative energies and the creation of sacred space. Most practitioners use the smoke of sage or sweetgrass in the form of smudge braids or sticks, which are bundles tied together and lit. However, one can also use herbs in a bowl, burn incense sticks or resins, or use sprays based on herbs.

Exercise: Cleansing

1 **Call spirit (*see* next page).**

2 **Burn sage or other herbs.**

3 **Use the smoke to firstly cleanse your aura and then walk around the space, stating an intent such as 'I am purifying this space, asking the smoke to take away negative energies and infuse it with sacred energy.'**

INVITING THE SACRED: CALLING SPIRIT

Bringing a sense of the sacred back into our lives happens organically when we start to walk a shamanic path, but in shamanism we also actively strive for it. Shamans, although they know their craft and have refined their skills, always call to the spirits and request their help before beginning their work and in their daily lives.

'Living in relationship with spirit is a uniquely personal journey. It means awakening to the sacredness in every moment and all forms of life.'

ANON

In our calls we also include specific forces that we wish to help or acknowledge. Examples are ancestral spirits, personal guides and power animals, certain nature spirits, or energies such as the feminine and masculine. But at the beginning of your shamanic path, a simple, heartfelt call is sufficient.

Exercise: A Basic Spirit Call

The following is a basic call, which can be used for all undertakings. You can use this, for example, to infuse your day with spirit in the morning.

1 Stand and centre yourself. Turn into the directions you are calling, accompany your call with a drum beat if you wish.

- **EAST:** 'I call the powers of the East. The spirits of the sun, of fire, light, illumination and creativity.'
- **SOUTH:** 'I call the spirits of the South. The spirits of water, the plant kingdom, of trust and flow.'
- **WEST:** 'I call the powers of the West. The spirits of Earth, of the deep, of introspection and our earth dream.'
- **NORTH:** 'I call the spirits of the North. The spirits of air, of our relations the animals, of wisdom and discernment.'

2 Turn in a circle and, with both arms outstretched, say out loud:

ALL THERE IS: 'I call all there is above and all there is below and Great Spirit to be with me and support me during this day. I pray that whatever I do and create is for the higher good of all of life.'

A SEAT FOR SPIRIT: THE SHAMANIC ALTAR

A shamanic altar is a physical home for spirit forces, functioning as a bridge between the worlds. The objects on a shamanic altar, at their most potent, hold the energy and power of that which they represent. Altars can be portable or fixed, used indoors or outdoors.

People on a shamanic path usually have a permanent, personal altar in their space, which holds their spiritual intent and is a focal point for the sacred in their lives. Altars assist in all spiritual undertakings, be they meditation, rituals, ceremonies, quests, journeys or healing.

Altars often have a basic structure, with objects that symbolize this structure, such as the four directions of the wheel – the East, South, West and North – but they are by no means static. They are living creations, adjusted to the work we do, our own development and the spirits we want to honour, attract or represent for a period of time.

Exercise: Create a Basic Altar

- **A CLOTH:** Use a piece of fabric that is beautiful and meaningful to you.
- **A CENTREPIECE:** Most people use a candle, signifying the children's fire or eternal life.
- **THE FOUR DIRECTIONS OF THE WHEEL:** Leaving some distance around the centrepiece, represent the four directions (I use four crystals, one for each direction).
- **THE FOUR ELEMENTS:** I also include the four elements of earth, air, fire and water in my basic structure (represent them in a way that works for you).

Altars should be created meditatively and with intent. Call spirit (*see* page 69) and, before you put each piece on the altar, infuse it with your intent and the spirit of what it represents. Hold the piece in your hands, breathe deeply, close your eyes and say, 'I dedicate this to the spirit of ... I am calling the spirit of .... to reside in it.' When you have created your altar, you can smudge it or rattle the energies into the altar space. Finish by thanking spirit and ask for your altar to be blessed.

NATURE: A WILD SACRED WEB OF LIFE

There can be no shamanic practice and path without the connection to nature. In shamanic terms, humans are dangerously out of balance.

By seeing ourselves as separate from and superior to nature we have lost the direct experience of the divine in creation and the teachings of nature that deepen our understanding of ourselves and what life is about. In shamanism we assume that many of the ecological, psychological and spiritual ailments of our time arise from this separation, and so we offer ways to re-embed ourselves within nature.

'All life is sacred and all creation related. What we do affects the whole universe.'

SMILING BEAR, CHEROKEE CLAN

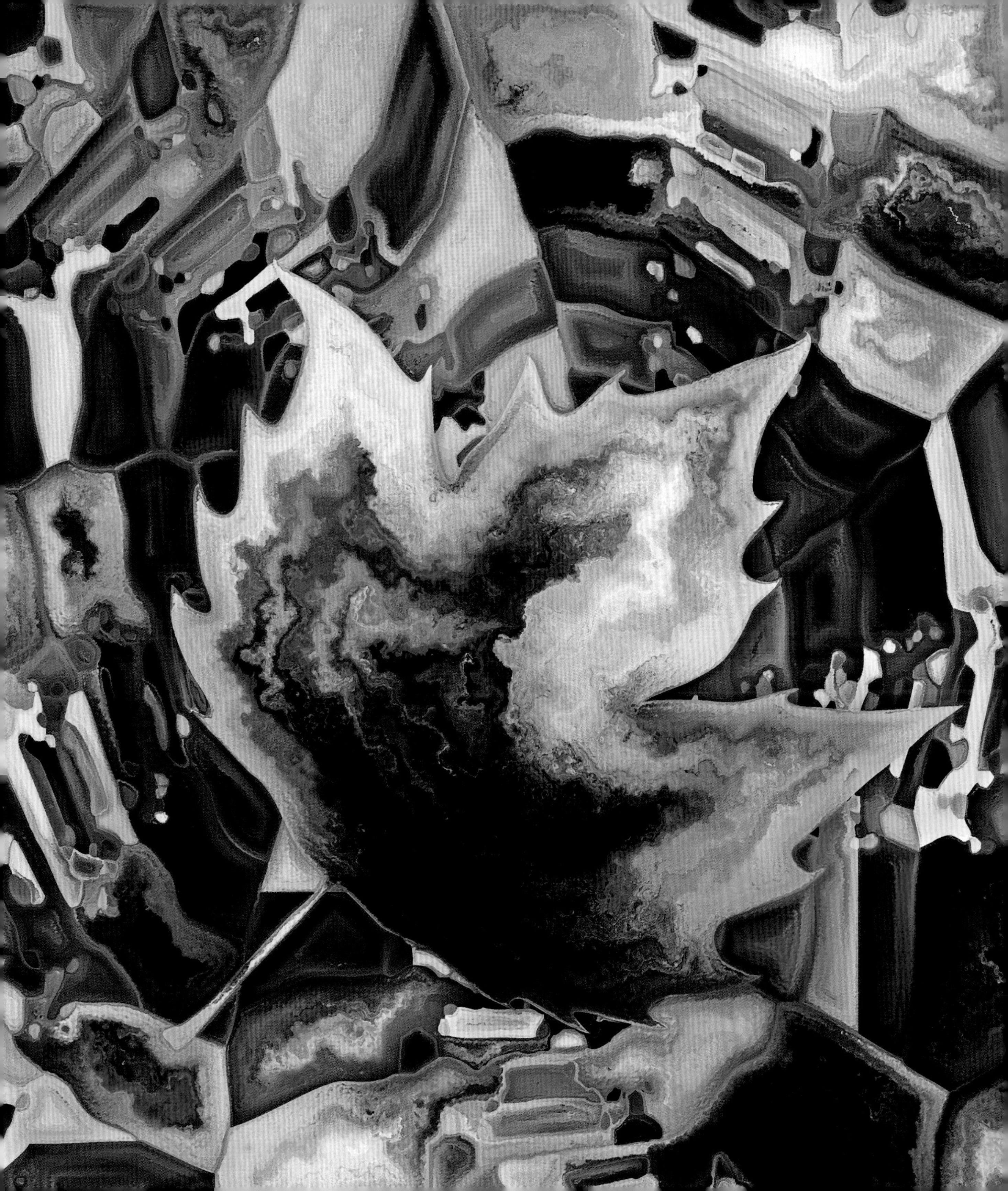

Shamanism teaches that life and the sacred can be directly experienced in nature and understood through observation and communication with the spirit(s) of nature. Once we experience the spiritual dimensions of nature, we realize that this spiritual dimension is also within us, and our consciousness expands in dramatic ways:

- **We understand** on a deep level that everything in the web that forms life on this earth is not only interrelated but as it derives from the same underlying spiritual field, it is equally sacred. This recognition leads inherently to an appreciation of life and to a desire to help it thrive, rather than exploit it for personal and collective gain.

- **We recognize** that our earth soul is indeed wild and therefore needs to spend time in nature and tune into the natural world for its nourishment. Every time we connect with nature in a sacred way, we reinforce the sacred within us, nurture our soul and give ourselves a chance to experience 'being home' in the sense that we feel embedded again within all of creation, rather than separate.

- **We appreciate** the shamanic notion that the disturbing levels of anxiety disorders and depression found in society, coupled with a sense of meaninglessness and powerlessness, are directly connected with our separation from nature and the starving of our earth souls. Recent research confirms that people of all age groups feel emotionally more alive and stable, more peaceful

and compassionate, and less anxious and hopeless after spending time in nature.

- **We realize** that what indigenous teachings call the 'right way to live' is about living in harmony and in balance with the natural laws. This means respecting the preciousness of all life, giving back whenever we take something, honouring the spirits within nature, contributing positively to the underlying energetic spiritual field and striving to live in a way that sustains creation.

The Shamanic Nature Repertoire

The shamanic repertoire for connecting with nature, expanding consciousness, healing ourselves and nourishing our earth souls is vast. Shamanic

Exercise: Experience the Sacred in Nature

1 Go outside and find a place that feels right, preferably under a tree or by a river.

2 Call spirit (*see* page 69).

3 Sit down and take a few deep breaths.

4 Touch: Touch the ground and feel it beneath you; breathe it in.

5 See: Look around you; let your eyes defocus and 'see' the vibrations, the fields, the beauty.

6 Listen: Become aware of the sounds and the subtle quietness underneath it all.

7 Feel: Feel the air and the space around you.

8 Now close your eyes and imagine that you are seen by Mother Nature.

9 Experience yourself as one of her children, experience her loving embrace.

10 Tune into the sacredness of this moment in nature.

11 Tune into the sacredness of your earth soul.

12 Breathe deeply and connect the outer with the inner, the sacredness within nature with your earth soul.

practitioners spend time in nature in order to communicate and merge with nature spirits, their allies and helpers and to tune into nature's sacredness. They will spend time in nature for inspiration and learning, re-energizing their powers, questing for vision, tuning into the natural rhythms and cycles, and attempting healing work within the underlying energetic fields.

'Shamanism brings us back to the original beauty, which is witnessed in nature.'

DON OSCAR MIRO-QUESADA

Everybody on a shamanic path can learn how to connect with the spirit essences that underlie nature's manifested forms, such as plants, trees, mountains, rivers, stars and planets, as well as with the elements of fire, water, earth and air. Much ceremonial work in shamanism takes place outside, often around fires or near water. Examples include the sweat lodge, medicine wheel ceremonies, and seasonal, moon and medicine plant ceremonies. Nature awareness walks, meditation, deep listening, initiations (such as the burial of the warrior), wilderness camps and pilgrimages to sacred sites are all part of the shamanic nature repertoire, as are vision quests and trance dance ceremonies.

ANCESTOR CONNECTIONS MATTER

In indigenous cultures and within most of shamanism it is believed that the ancestors not only gave us the precious gift of life but, once in spirit, also hold humanity's memories and wisdom.

It is therefore essential to be in contact with the ancestors, acknowledge their importance, be grateful to them, utilize their guidance, learn from their mistakes and create change.

'Walking, I am listening. Suddenly all my ancestors are behind me. Be still, they say. Watch and listen. You are the result of the love of thousands.'

LINDA HOGAN

Ancestors, in a traditional sense, are people who have lived before us and are now in spirit. They can be the ones that share our bloodlines, or are connected to us via place and, in some teachings, the ones that form part of our soul groups.

In shamanic thinking, the disconnection from ancestors in modern societies has produced many harmful developments for our individual and collective psyche:

- **We are isolated individuals** without deeper roots. This contributes to the suffering of our souls and to our disconnection from the whole.
- **Disconnected from our ancestors**, we have lost sight of future generations and of our duty to leave them a habitable and nurturing world.
- **We are depriving ourselves** of the help and guidance from our ancestors in spirit.

Reconnecting with Our Ancestors

Shamanic practitioners are connected to ancestors, honour them and ask them for help and guidance. If we want to expand our consciousness, become more rooted and begin to walk a shamanic path, connecting with our ancestors is one of the first, vital steps. Rooting us into a wider field of past, present and future, our ancestors provide us with easily accessible guidance, help and wisdom because they have a special energetic relationship with us.

Exercise: Ancestral Altar and Communication

One way to honour your ancestors, connect and communicate with them is to make a small shrine or represent them on your altar. You will need:

1 A cloth that is beautiful to you.

2 A candle or candles.

3 An image of one or a group of your own ancestors or an image of a site/ landscape that has a strong connection with your ancestors, or both.

4 Include an offering of honey, sweet things or a nice dish of grain or tobacco – ancestors like to be nourished.

5 Put objects on the altar that have a connection with your ancestors, such as stones, earth or something that one of your ancestors used professionally, such as a needle, pen or cloth.

6 Be creative. Your intent in building the shrine is to honour and communicate with your ancestors.

7 Now, smudge the space or burn incense.

8 Sit down and take a few deep breaths, imagine your ancestors hearing you and begin your communication saying, 'I honour those who came before me and thank you for giving me life.' Listen with all your senses and keep communicating.

THE SHAMANIC JOURNEY TO THE SPIRIT WORLDS

The contemporary shamanic journey provides a way to travel into the lower, upper and middle worlds. It is used for a variety of issues, all with the common aim of contributing to our connection with the spirit worlds, expanding our consciousness, and healing and evolving towards wholeness.

'Shamanic journeying is the inner art of travelling to the invisible worlds beyond ordinary reality to retrieve information for change in any area of your life – from spirituality and health to work and relationships.'

SANDRA INGERMAN

Generally, shamans journey to connect, communicate and work with spirit and to connect with their power animals, spirit guides and other spirits. They travel to find out the source of an issue and the path of the resolution. They might receive guidance about which ritual or ceremony to perform, which herbs to use, which spirits to get involved or which soul parts to bring back. The journey is furthermore used for divination and different forms of energetic healing within the energetic realms of those worlds.

In a more therapeutic shamanic context, we can journey to find something we need to let go of, retrieve split-off parts (soul retrieval), reveal the cause of a problem, discover solutions, heal emotional wounding and more. We can also journey to learn about things, such as our task in this world, our shadow aspects, our spiritual selves, our connection with our ancestors, our essence qualities or our purpose.

How to Journey

The adapted journey most contemporary practitioners use was brought to the West by Michael Harner. It is 20–30 minutes long and usually accompanied by a steady drum rhythm that leads and holds the person in an altered state. Journeys can also be danced or attempted with other trance induction, such as guided visualizations or vibrations of gongs or rattles. The journey itself is an unfolding process. With the appropriate set-up, a clear intent, spirit being present and the help of power animals and/or guides, every journey unfolds as it is meant to.

When we journey our task is to be observant, aware and focused, and to let the journey unfold, reaching its natural conclusion. Journeying works on an energetic as well as mental/emotional level, often producing the required changes, answers and information, but sometimes we also employ integrative techniques or do further work after journeying.

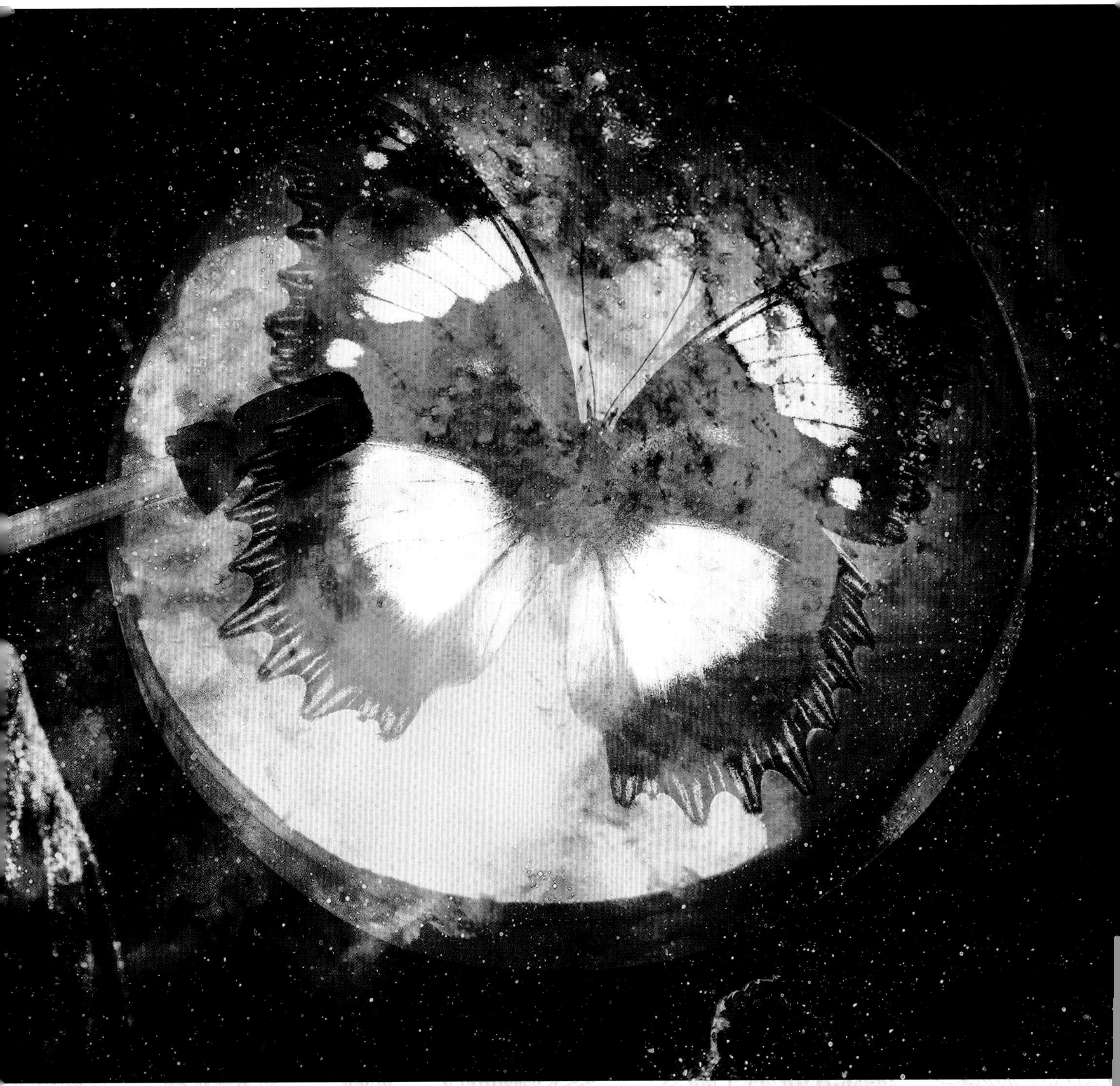

You can use the journey to connect with an upper world guide. Your intent will be 'I journey to the upper world to meet a spirit guide.' Imagine that you travel upwards, through many increasingly etheric and vague layers. When you meet a being, ask if he/she is your guide. Be with them. Observe. Be guided. Ask questions.

Exercise: Connect with a Power Animal

1 Download the 20-minute journey drumming recording from my website www.christamackinnon.com

2 Call spirit (*see* page 69).

3 Lie down. Be comfortable.

4 Switch on the drumming download.

5 State your intent three times: 'I am journeying to the lower world to meet my power animal.'

6 Imagine yourself travelling downwards; you can imagine going through the roots of a tree or through a hole in the ground or descending into a cave.

7 You will arrive in a landscape.

8 Explore your landscape, walk around, notice details.

9 At one point an animal will come to you. If not, state your intent again.

10 Walk away from the animal.

11 You need to meet the same animal three times.

12 Ask: 'Are you my power animal?' If the answer is yes: be with the animal, observe, let the animal lead. Find out its specific qualities, its medicine for you.

13 When you hear the drum beat change: imagine that you come back up, bringing the animal with you.

14 Write your journey down. Write about the qualities of your power animal.

CEREMONY & RITUAL

Ceremony and ritual are used to connect and work with the different energies within and around us, with spirit and the sacred. At their most powerful they form bridges between ordinary realms and the realms of the unseen, between our body-mind and our soul-spirit and between the sacred and the mundane. In the process they integrate different aspects of our multidimensional personal and transpersonal selves, thereby creating harmony between them.

Ceremony and ritual have always been used for rites of passage, for blessings, initiations, dedications, cleansing, for the shaman's flight and journeys to the Otherworlds, for giving something back to the earth, to tune into nature's cycles and for questing vision, healing and advice. They also lend themselves to resolve issues, speaking or hearing the truth, resolving unfinished business, celebrating an achievement, giving thanks, sending out prayers, releasing or giving away fear, anger

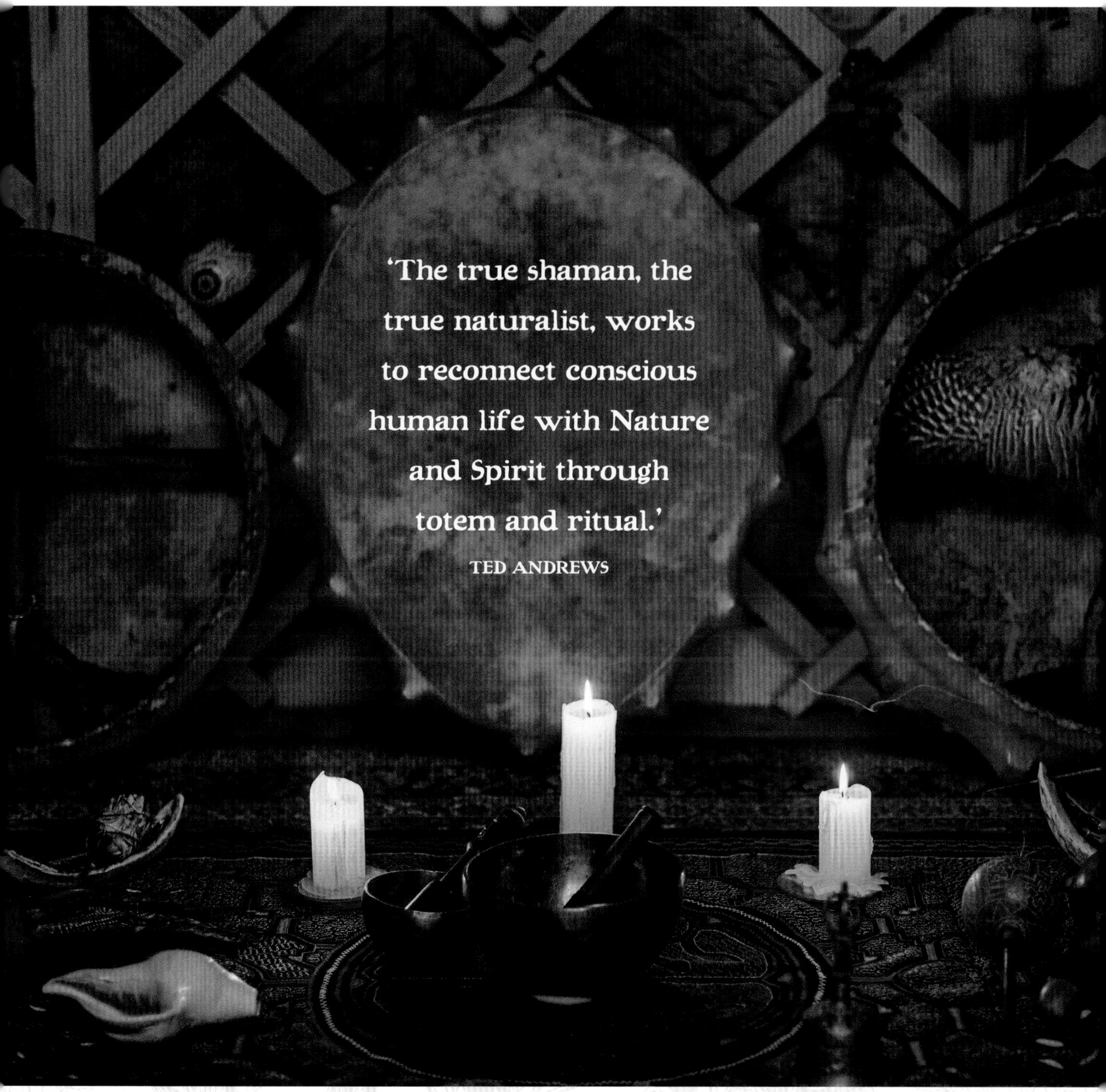
'The true shaman, the
true naturalist, works
to reconnect conscious
human life with Nature
and Spirit through
totem and ritual.'
TED ANDREWS

or grief, or to calling in something that we want to attract. No matter what the purpose of a ceremony, participating in ceremony is healing and often quite transformational.

Traditional Ceremonies and Rituals

Traditional ceremonies, whether they are rituals in the sense that they have been used in the same form repeatedly, or more flexible leaving room for creativity, are often long and intense affairs and can be found worldwide. The ceremonies of the North American indigenous tribes are well-known, such as the Sun Dance ceremony, the Pow-Wow and the Sweat Lodge. Fire ceremonies are practised in various forms around the world. Familiar to the northern hemisphere are the Solstice and Equinox ceremonies that honour and attune us to the cycles of nature. Healing ceremonies come in many forms such as the Navajo healing ritual utilizing sand mandalas, and the Gabonese healing ceremony, now used to address drug dependency. Others include ancestral ceremonies practised all over Africa, the Americas and in the Far East, trance dance ceremonies for connection and harmony between the people and spirit, and of course the increasingly popular plant ceremonies, such as mushroom, peyote or ayahuasca ceremonies, practised mainly in South America.

How and Why Ceremony Works

In shamanic ceremony we enter into a sacred, symbolic enactment of an intent, within a sacred space and with spirit present. The symbolism used has meaning for our deeper self and our soul, whilst the intense enactment takes us effortlessly into a higher state of consciousness, eliciting powerful responses within the individual psyche and the whole group, thus producing connection, harmony, healing, change and manifestation.

Ceremony and ritual often involve the community or is done in groups, but we also use them with individual clients and for ourselves. For example, I conduct a brief 'greeting and blessing' ceremony every morning to connect with nature, spirit and my own deeper self and I often use a small fire ceremony when clients need to 'let go' of something.

Exercise: Connect with Your Spirit Circle

This ceremony is best done in nature (under a tree or near water), but can also be done inside.

1 Create or mark a circle with stones, crystals or branches.
2 Call spirit (*see* page 69).
3 Light a candle and put it in the middle of the circle.
4 Sit in front of the candle, looking at it until your eyes defocus.
5 Close your eyes and imagine that you walk into a grove and see the candle.
6 Walk towards the candle and sit down, facing the candle.
7 Ask for the spirit helpers – ancestors, power animals and guides – you need to communicate with at this moment in time to join you. Speak this aloud a few times.
8 Be still, breathe and observe. See, feel, intuit the spirit allies joining you. They might be walking towards you or you might sense them sitting around you.
9 Start the communication by saying 'Thank you for being here with me. I have come to honour you. Let the communication/event unfold.
10 The allies in your spirit circle 'disappear' when 'all is said and done' or when you begin to thank them.
11 Finish by thanking your spirit allies. Open your yes. Blow out the candle.

DANCING INTO ECSTASY: SHAMANIC TRANCE DANCE

Trance dancing is one of the most enjoyable and deep-reaching ways of entering altered states and connecting to the spirit worlds. It is a way of creating a free flow of energy through the body and letting the physical and emotional express themselves.

At the blissful peak when 'the dancer becomes the dance' we experience a state that is beyond mind and are able to connect with our very essence and the vibrational fields around us. In the process we let go of tension, our egos and stuck emotional and physical energies, simultaneously gaining insights and finding balance, making trance dancing a healing tool.

> **'In the beginning we all danced.... Our ancestors danced until they disappeared in the dance, till they felt the full force of spirit unleashing their souls.'**
>
> GABRIELLE ROTH

Dance Traditions Around the World

All our tribal ancestors loved to dance and many old traditions and their spiritual components and meanings have been kept alive around the world. Examples range from the sun dances of the North American Plains and

Canada to the whirling dances of the Sufis in Turkey and from the ritualistic dances of the South American tribes to the mask dances of the Balinese and the voodoo trance dances of Haiti. In Africa, all the remaining tribes and their medicine men and women dance themselves into trances, as do the Huichol of Mexico when they ingest peyote, and the Mongolian, Nepalese, Siberian and Korean shamans when they connect with spirit.

Intense trance dancing is usually facilitated by rhythmic drumming that becomes increasingly faster. Some shamans, when dancing for divination, information, prophecy or healing, also use singing and chanting

to connect with and to convey messages from spirits. During ecstatic dances some shamans express fights with malicious spirits when they dance for the healing of a person or the community, or for spirit extraction. Others open themselves to possession to become a vessel for spirits, which enter their body/mind, expressing themselves directly through movement and voice. Powerful spirit possessions can be seen in Africa, South America, Mongolia, Siberia or Korea, for example. These dramatic affairs are not for the faint-hearted but, if genuine, they show the extreme abilities of traditional shamans.

'If you want to give birth to your true self, you are going to have to dig deep down into that body of yours and let your soul howl. Your feet will take you where you need to go.'

GABRIELLE ROTH

Contemporary Ecstatic Dance Practices

Contemporary shamanism uses traditional practices but has also adapted trance dance in various ways, all of them aimed at connecting with spirit, with our essence and to facilitate physical, mental and emotional healing and transformation. Shamanic trance dancing, chakra dancing and '5Rhythms' dancing are not only practices, but can become a spiritual path. All of them produce remarkable results by enabling people to move energy, discharge stored-up and blocked emotions, free their minds and connect with their souls and spirit.

If dancing attracts you, find one of the following in the area you live. Dancing might be your path.

Contemporary Shamanic Trance Dance

Like everything in shamanism, we use trance dance with intent and purpose. It is mostly done in groups in a sacred, ceremonial space and follows a preliminary preparations phase, in which every dancer formulates their intent for the dance. Dancers are accompanied by drummers of African djembes or specific, rhythm-based music, and they usually dance for between one and four hours, until they lose themselves completely in the dance and sink to the ground. During the dance they encounter images, visions, emotions, memories and insights

corresponding to their intent, which are processed adaptively during the dance.

5Rhythms Dancing

5Rhythms dancing is a combination of shamanic trance dance, Eastern philosophy and contemporary dance movements. It is a semi-structured spiritual dance practice founded by Gabrielle Roth, who described it as a moving meditation of ecstatic dance, which opens the heart and frees the mind. It leads us from whatever is happening right now on a journey of moving and discharging physical and mental/emotional blockages into a place of stillness and bliss. In the process it connects us to the essence of our soul and spirit, the source of all inspiration, possibilities and potential.

Chakra Dancing

Focusing on the energy centres of the body, chakra dancing was originally inspired by tribal and spiritual dancing from around the world. It blends free-flowing movements with specific frequencies of beats and sounds, which are connected to the seven energetic centres (chakras) of the body. It is generally based on the idea that emotional, mental, physical and spiritual blockages occur in the cells and muscles of the body, manifesting as images, memories, hunches, feelings, intuitions, aches and pains. Dancing through the vibrations of each centre gives them a chance to be integrated or released.

THE POWER OF THE DREAM STATE: LUCID DREAMING

Shamans are often called 'dreamers', with the expression 'dreaming' being used to describe the trance states shamans use to access the various worlds as well as the work they do in these worlds.

It can also mean the dreams experienced during sleep and the shaman's power to interpret them, dream with intent and utilize lucid dreaming for their work. Many shamanic cultures believe that we are the 'dreamers' of our reality, that what we experience

daily with our senses is the manifested reality of the underlying, individual and collective dreams, and can therefore be experienced, explored, altered and shaped from within the dreamscape.

'Everyone who dreams has a little bit of the shaman in them.'

ROBERT MOSS

Dreaming is still practised in indigenous cultures around the world. The Shuar (Ecuador), Guarani (Brazil) and Mapuche (Chile) consider the 'true self 'of every human being as living within their dreams. They share dreams, discuss them and act upon them, as do the people of the Australian First Nations. The Orang Aoli, the aboriginal people of Malaysia, are known as a dreaming culture and most African tribes also put much emphasis on dreams. Lee Irwin, who researched the dream traditions of 23 groups of American Indians Plains People, found dreaming very much alive and learned that the shaman's art is closely linked with the art of dreaming.

It is a general consensus in all strands of shamanism that dreaming is a potent state in which underlying energetic realities/spirit worlds can be accessed. Shamanic cultures have a wealth of knowledge concerning dream worlds and all shamanic practitioners pay attention to dreams, especially when they are 'big dreams', concerning major life events or shifts, prophetic dreams or dreams that convey essential information for the individual or the community that need to be acted upon.

Intentional Lucid Dreaming

Whilst everybody in shamanism pays attention to dreams, dream shamans have the power to dream intentionally and lucidly and work within their dreams. In intentional lucid dreaming we are awake whilst dreaming a dream that we have requested before going to sleep. It is a state where our normal waking awareness and our dream-state perception meet. With this dual awareness and control within the dream, the shaman can access energetic powers, information, insight and help, and has the power to create energetically with the aim of manifestation in the waking world.

Lucid dreaming with intent is a skill that requires training, practice and strong ethics.

Dream shamans, often called to this work by spirit, have to master many levels of dreaming. Ruby Modesto, a medicine woman of the Desert Cahuilla Indians, trained and worked for decades to master 13 levels of dreaming. She decides where she wants to go and what she wants to experience or be shown. During the first lucid dream, she intends what she wants to dream in the second dream; in the second dream she intends the third dream, and so on. The power of lucid dreaming is expressed by the renowned contemporary indigenous American healer and 'dream walker' Rolling Thunder, who suggests that lucid dreaming is a more reliable source of visions than mind-altering plants.

What We Can Do in Lucid Dreaming

Lucid dreaming expands consciousness and can be used for almost everything shamanic. We can directly meet with guides and teachers, receive learning and guidance, and work energetically in the dream state to manifest healing and change. Shamanic practitioners might ask for information about an ailment and its required healing method, which they then either perform in the dream state or later in the waking state. They might ask for a prophetic dream, or for vision and insight into an issue, or to meet and be taught by specific spirits, teachers and guides. They might intend dreams about lost souls, which they will guide to other realms during the lucid dream, or to counteract negative forces within the energetic realm, which they will eradicate or transform within the dream.

'Remember that thoughts are not original, brilliant, or creative – your instinct, ideas, and ability to dream are.

ALBERTO VILLOLDO

To become a lucid dreamer is a worthwhile undertaking. It can be learned and practised and will lead you into magical realms, expand your power, provide you with a powerful medicine and assist you in being the co-creator of your life.

Exercise: Lucid Dreaming

Lucid dreaming in a shamanic sense needs training and practice. Here are the first steps that will assist you:

1 DEVELOP DREAM RECALL: Before going to sleep repeat the following sentence: 'I am going to dream. When I wake up I will remember a dream.' Then, instantly upon waking, write the dream you remember into your dream journal.

2 DREAMING WITH INTENT: Once you have practised and strengthened your recall abilities you can proceed to the next step. Before falling asleep, repeat the following sentence: 'Tonight I am going to dream about [insert a subject]. I will remember this dream when I wake up'. Again, when you wake up, write the dream down.

Most people need to do these exercises over a period of time, but some of us are natural dreamers in the sense that we remember our dreams easily. Once you are sufficiently competent in intentional dreaming, I would advise you to do a course or at least read more about 'lucid dreaming with intent' before you attempt it.

SO MUCH MORE & SO MUCH FURTHER

This book offers a brief introduction, but has by no means completely covered shamanism. Much could still be said.

I have left out the many direct shamanic energy healing practices, as they need to be experienced to comprehend them. Shamanic practitioners use sound vibrations of drums, rattles and voice, smoke, herbs and their breath, bodies and hands to extract negative energies and to infuse positive ones.

I also omitted spirit extractions, based on the assumption that malevolent spirits can invade the body and the energy fields of people, needing to be extracted. And I excluded psychopomp work, which is employed to help souls cross over into other dimensions. Both need advanced training and skill sets.

Vision quests, wilderness work, soul retrieval, initiation rituals and out-of-body travelling were only mentioned briefly and I also excluded complete systems, such as the magnificent medicine wheel teachings.

With plant medicine ceremonies now much in demand, I want to mention them briefly before I close, as they are literally mind-blowing. Psychoactive mushrooms and plants such as

ayahuasca, ibogaine, San Pedro cactus and peyote have been part of shamanism for as long as we know. Such naturally occurring medicines are seen as great teachers, as gifts from Mother Earth to help us to expand consciousness, heal and connect and work with the spirit worlds. They open and interconnect normally closed and separated neural pathways, granting us access to profound visionary states, unimaginable worlds and much-needed healing. Ingested at the right time, with the right set-up and within a sacred context and skilled facilitation they can work their magic in profound ways. However, they shouldn't be taken lightly, as they can also overwhelm the mind, body and psyche – and one needs to be aware that they are classified as illegal substances in some countries.

No matter what I have included in this book or left out, when it comes to shamanism, the most important ingredient is exploration and experience. Shamanism is, after all, often described as a spiritual path of direct experience, as opposed to religions or spiritual pathways that have set teachings, beliefs, priests and rules. The best way to start to explore and experience shamanism is to choose something you feel drawn to. Once you begin to work with an individual practitioner or join a group, workshop or training, your specific path will unfold and teachings will come your way, because what you seek is also seeking you. I wish you much joy on your journey.

RESOURCES

There is a wealth of resources about shamanism, including books, websites, social media groups, workshops, training courses and events worldwide. I have included here some books, covering various areas of shamanism, and card decks. Please contact me via my website http://www.christamackinnon.com if you would like specific recommendations about courses, events, social media groups and websites.

Books

***The Gift of Shamanism: Visionary Power, Ayahuasca Dreams, and Journeys to Other Realms* by Itzhak Beery**
In this invaluable and fascinating book, Beery describes his personal journey from businessman to shamanic practitioner.

***Fire in the Head* by Tom Cowan**
A book that gives you much insight into Celtic shamanism as well as stories and exercises.

***The Way of the Shaman* by Michael Harner**
A not-to-miss classic within the field of shamanism. Its publication led to the term and teachings of 'core shamanism', which are now widely used.

***Shamanic Journeying: A Beginner's Guide* and *The Book of Ceremony*, both by Sandra Ingerman**
Written by one of the most renowned American core-shamanic teachers, these are full of insights from Sandra's shamanic work and practical exercises.

***Shamanism Made Easy: Awaken and Develop the Shamanic Force Within* by Christa Mackinnon**
A best-selling all-round introduction, this book provides insight into most areas of shamanism and many step-by-step exercises.

***Shamanism and Spirituality in Therapeutic Practice* by Christa Mackinnon**
The first ground-breaking book, combining contemporary therapy with shamanism. Essential reading for anybody who is interested in both.

***Food of the Gods: The Search for the Original Tree of Knowledge* by Terence McKenna and *Breaking Open the Head: A Psychedelic Journey into the Heart of Contemporary Shamanism* by Daniel Pinchbeck**
Both are highly recommended if you are interested in psychoactive plant medicines.

***Black Elk Speaks: Being the Life Story of a Holy Man of the Oglala Sioux* by John Neihardt**
This is an amazing book if you want to hear the wisdom of one of the greatest early Indigenous American teachers.

***Nature and the Human Soul* and *Wild Mind*, both by Bill Plotkin**
These dive deeply into the connection of human psyche, mind and nature, including stories from Bill's time in the wilderness.

***An Encyclopedia of Shamanism* (Vol I and II) by Christina Pratt**
This is an invaluable resource providing definitions and brief descriptions of the vast array of shamanic practices worldwide.

***The Medicine Bag: Shamanic Rituals and Ceremony for Personal Transformation* by Don Jose Ruiz**
Written by a renowned shaman of the Toltec tradition, this is a how-to book about rituals and ceremony, dreaming, nature work and more.

***Sky Shamans of Mongolia: Meetings with Remarkable Healers* by Kevin Turner**
This is worth reading if you are interested in Mongolia's old, revived traditions.

Card Decks

***Native Spirit Oracle Cards* by Denise Linn**
Denise is a member of the Cherokee Nation. The cards focus on nature spirits and teachings. They are accompanied by a small booklet, providing interpretations, ideas of how to use the cards and practical follow-up exercises.

***Medicine Cards: The Discovery of Power Through the Ways of Animals* by Jamie Sams and David Carson**
These are the classics and very widely used in the West. They come with a comprehensive book, explaining the meaning and origin of the teaching's beautiful ways.

Workshops, Training Courses and Social Media

You will find shamanic workshops, training courses and events, as well as information about our medicine woman training, on my website:
www.christamackinnon.com

I can also recommend specific workshops and courses by other teachers and practitioners and point you in the direction of websites and social media groups addressing specific subjects within shamanism.

ACKNOWLEDGMENTS

Author Biographies

Christa Mackinnon (author, MSc Psych, DFC, PgDhyp, DipITEC, MBSCH), a former psychologist, therapist, university lecturer and international trainer, now works as a therapeutic shaman and shamanic teacher. Christa was initiated by indigenous shamans in Ecuador and Brazil, and trained with shamans and spiritual teachers worldwide. Her training organization 'Bridging the Worlds', provides courses for therapeutic professionals, combining indigenous spiritual teaching with Western psychological approaches, a subject she also writes, lectures and talks widely about. Christa also facilitates shamanic workshops for lay people and is the co-founder of the 'Modern Medicine Woman Training School' where she provides training courses for modern medicine women. She is the author of three books about shamanism. **www.christamackinnon.com**

Itzhak Beery (foreword) is a best-selling author of three books, a leading shamanic teacher, healer, speaker, community activist and trip leader. Since 1995, Itzhak has bridged the spiritual and practical wisdom his indigenous and Western teachers entrusted him with. His Quechua teacher initiated him in Ecuador into the Circle of 24 Yachaks, and he has also received initiation from Amazonian Kanamari Pajè. He is the founder of ShamanPortal.org and The Andes Summit, and co-founder of the New York Shamanic Circle. Itzhak is on the faculties of major spiritual centres worldwide. He received the Ambassador for Peace Award from The Universal Peace Federation and the UN. He lives in New York City. **www.itzhakbeery.com**

Picture Credits

Special thanks to all the artists who have contributed artwork to this book, in page order: *Visionary Man*, *Awakening Spirit*, *Wisdom of the Divine Emerging*, *Metamorphic Awakening* by **© Kim Dreyer**, www.kimdreyerart.com 7, 8, 18, 67; *Shamanic Symphony* by **© Anderson Debernardi** 13; **© Vestia Von Geist**, www.thegildedgrove.com 21; **© Darya Laryukhina** 31; **© Gautam Nair**, www.shadedmirrors.com 38; **© Laura Csajagi** 41; **© Christa Mackinnon** 48; **© Rebecca Sinz** 49; **© Roger Vincent Hitchcock**, illustrator, facebook @rvh99 57. Courtesy of **Pixabay** and © the following: Anke Sundermeier 20; romainriere 33. Courtesy of **Rex Features (Shutterstock Editorial)**/NARENDRA SHRESTHA/EPA-EFE: 24. Courtesy of **Shutterstock.com** and © the following: Angelina De Sol 1 & throughout; Peratek 2 & throughout; Jozef Klopacka 3c & front cover, 4, 9, 19, 25, 32, 36, 50, 61, 62, 68, 71, 83, 86, 91, 93, 94; marina shin 6; Zolotarevs 11, 76, 100; Bruce Rolff 12, 39, 52, 53, 113; CW Pix 14, 28; agsandrew 17, 59, 74, 75, 114, 116, 121; Valerii_M 22; Pises Tungittipokai 23; Dmitry Chulov 26; clicksdemexico 29; Anna september 30; 1008 34; Fesleen 35; Mastak A 40; NextMarsMedia 42; Barandash Karandashich 43; Nikki Zalewski 45; Miriama Taneckova 46, 51, 54, 125; Oliver Denker 47; Aleksey Ignatenko 55; Mohamed Ali Elmeshad 56, 112; Zelenov Iurii 58; yulianas 63; Kertu 64, 106; Microgen 65, 81; Maridav 66; marcovarro 70; Charlie Blacker 72; Guido Vermeulen-Perdaen 77; Alex Tihonovs 78; Alex Tooth 79; Elina Leonova 80; Slava Gerj 84; Dmytro Rybin 85; Aretxiga 89 main; Karin Hildebrand Lau 89 inset; OLaLa Merkel 90, 128; Elena Ray 96, 101; samaliusfoto 97; Ammit Jack 98; Majna 99; Frame 18 Productions 102; Cassiohabib 103; Jim Parkin 104; mehmetcan 105; Roby1960 107; FreeProd33 108; An Vino 110; Golubovy 111; Matt Renaud 115; Harizma 118; Benjavisa Ruangvaree Art 120; Dana Toerien 123; OceanBlack 126.